I WONDER Why

Romans Wore Togas

and other questions about Rome

Fiona Macdonald

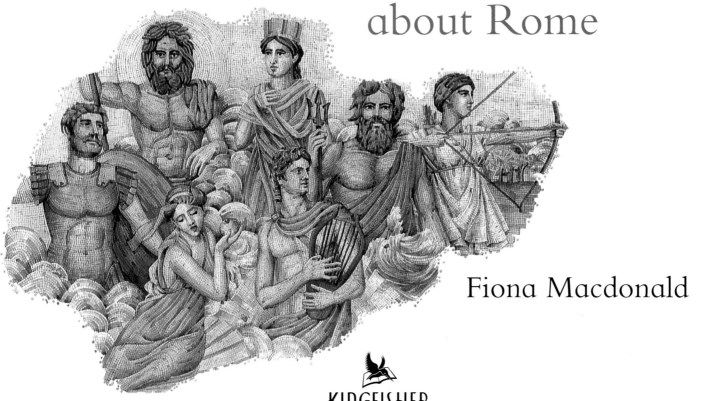

KINGFISHER
NEW YORK

First published 1997 by Kingfisher
This edition published 2012 by Kingfisher

Consultant: Dr. Paul Roberts

Distributed in the U.S. and Canada by Macmillan,
175 Fifth Ave., New York, NY 10010

Library of Congress Cataloging-in-Publication data has been
applied for.

ISBN: 978-0-7534-6794-7

Kingfisher books are available for special promotions and
premiums. For details contact: Special Markets Department,
Macmillan, 175 Fifth Ave., New York, NY 10010.

For more information, please visit www.kingfisherbooks.com

Printed in China
9 8 7 6 5 4 3 2 1
1TR/0612/UTD/WKT/140MA

Illustrations: Simone Bovi (Virgil Pomfret) 16–17; Peter Dennis
(Linda Rogers) 8–9, 28–29; Luigi Galante (Virgil Pomfret)
4–5, 18–19, 28–29; Christian Hook 22–23, 30–31; Tony
Kenyon (B.L. Kearley) all cartoons; Nicki Palin cover, 6–7,
14–15, 24–25; Claudia Saraceni 12–13; Rob Shone 30bl;
Thomas Trojer 20–21; David Wright (Kathy Jakeman) 10–11.

CONTENTS

Who were the Romans?

The Romans were people who came from Rome. About 2,000 years ago they became so powerful that they began to conquer the lands around them. By A.D. 100 they ruled a huge empire, and were one of the mightiest peoples in the ancient world.

Different parts of the empire had very different climates. Romans boiled in Egypt, where the summers were sweltering . . .

An old legend says that the city of Rome was first started by a man called Romulus. He and his twin brother Remus had been abandoned by their parents and were looked after by a wolf!

BRITAIN

Hadrian's Wall

London

FRANCE
(Gaul)

Lyon   Alps

SPAIN

Pyrenees

ITALY

Rome

Pompeii

Mediterranean Sea

Carthage

AFRICA

... but they shivered in the icy Swiss Alps and in northern Britain. These were the coldest places in the entire empire.

Did all the Romans live in Rome?

The city of Rome wasn't big enough for all of the Romans! All in all, there were about 50 million people in the empire, which stretched from Britain in the north to Africa in the south. Everyone in the empire was protected by Rome's armies, but had to obey Rome's laws.

THE ROMAN EMPIRE
100 A.D.

Caspian Sea

Black Sea

Constantinople

Athens · Ephesus

ASIA MINOR
· Antioch

SYRIA

ARABIA

Alexandria

EGYPT

Red Sea

N

3,000 miles

It would have taken almost 100 days to ride from one end of the empire to the other. It was a journey of over 3,000 Roman miles, (5,000 kilometers).

Who ruled Rome?

Over the years, Rome was ruled in three different ways: first by kings, then by a number of officials who were chosen by the people, and finally by emperors, who were really kings under a different name!

Some Roman emperors ruled wisely, but others did whatever they pleased . . .

Nero was mad and bad. Some people say he set fire to the city of Rome.

Hadrian visited every corner of the empire, and made it stronger.

Caligula wasted the riches of Rome. He believed he was a god.

Who was born free?

Roman citizens were. They were not only able to vote in elections, they also got free seats at the amphitheater and free use of the public baths. When times were hard, they got free loaves of bread, too!

Roman women did not have the same rights as men. They were not allowed to vote, and had to obey their husband or father. But that doesn't mean they always did!

Who slaved away for the Romans?

Most of the hard work in Rome was done by slaves. These men, women, and children were captured overseas, and then sold in the marketplace in Rome. They had to wear an identity tag with their master's name and address on it—just in case they got lost.

The first Roman emperor was called Augustus. He was advised by a group of wealthy men, called senators, who were used to running the army and the government.

Slaves were sometimes given their freedom after many years of good service, or if their master wanted to be kind.

When did the army use tortoises?

When Roman soldiers were advancing toward the enemy, they did a special trick called "the tortoise." They held their shields high above their heads to make a kind of shell. This protected them from enemy spears—but made it hard for them to see where they were going!

IV/VII/CIV

Dear Mom
Having an awful time.
The Barbarians are fierce and
I think the Centurion hates me.
Please send me V sesterces
for food.
Your loving son
Marcus xxx

Soldiers were often hungry and cold. Many of them wrote letters home asking for extra food and clothing.

Injured soldiers bandaged their wounds with cobwebs soaked in vinegar. This helped the soldiers, but wasn't so good for the spiders!

Which soldiers left home for 25 years?

Most soldiers had to stay in the army for 25 years. Those who were Roman citizens were luckier—they could leave after only 20 years! Soldiers had a hard life. They were far from home, and had to put up with danger, tough training, and harsh punishments.

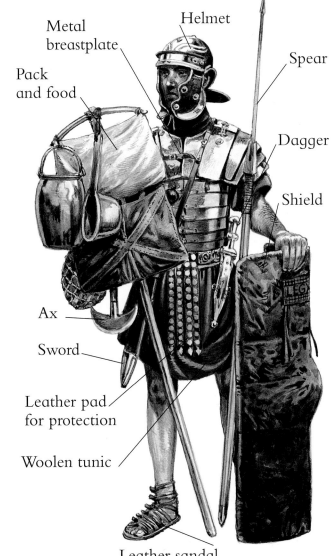

Metal breastplate
Helmet
Spear
Pack and food
Dagger
Shield
Ax
Sword
Leather pad for protection
Woolen tunic
Leather sandal

In warmer parts of the empire, soldiers didn't wear much under their tunics. But in chilly places they wore thick woolen underwear—just like the locals.

Who attacked the Romans with elephants?

Hannibal was the Spanish leader of the Carthaginians, a people from North Africa. He led a huge army and a herd of elephants across France and over the snow-covered Alps on a long march to Italy. In battle, the elephants charged at the Roman soldiers, who soon ran away in terror.

Queen Cleopatra of Egypt used her beauty and charm to fight against the Romans. She made two Roman commanders fall in love with her—Julius Caesar and Mark Antony.

In Britain, the Romans built Hadrian's Wall, which was 75 miles (120 kilometers) long. From its towers, they spied on tribes in Scotland to the north.

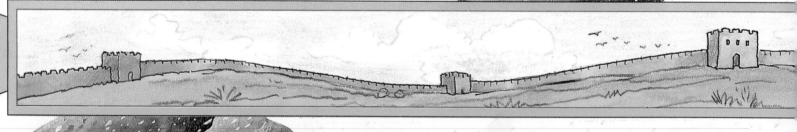

Forty thousand men and 37 elephants made the long, dangerous march from Spain across the Alps—the mountains in northern Italy. Sadly, many of them died from the cold along the way.

Which Roman guards went honk-honk-honk?

A flock of holy geese lived among the temples on Rome's Capitoline Hill. One dark night, a fierce tribe called the Gauls were planning an attack. They crept up the hill, but were heard by the geese, who honked a loud warning and saved the citizens of Rome.

Who cut the Romans to pieces?

When the Romans attacked Britain, they had to face fierce warriors like Queen Boudicca. Legend says she fixed sharp knives to the wheels of her chariot and then drove right into the lines of soldiers. Ouch!

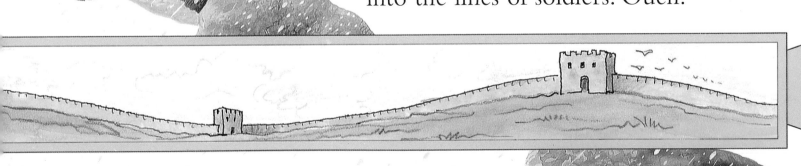

Who did the Romans worship?

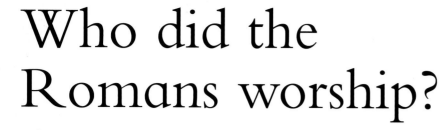

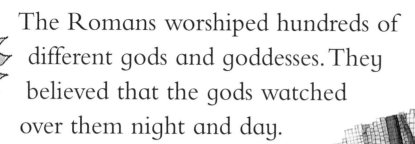

The Romans worshiped hundreds of different gods and goddesses. They believed that the gods watched over them night and day. Some looked after the earth and the sea. Some cared for special groups such as doctors, merchants, or soldiers. And others watched over the different parts of people's lives—their health, beauty, or love life.

Jupiter, king of the gods

The Romans thought that snakes brought good luck, so they painted them on their walls.

Mars, god of war

The Romans believed that spirits lived in the rivers, woods, and fields. They protected wild animals and the plants that grew there.

Venus, goddess of love

Juno, queen of the gods

Sick Romans prayed to the gods to cure them. If they got better, they left a thank-you present in the temple—a little statue of the part of their body that had been cured.

Neptune, god of the sea

Diana, goddess of the Moon and of hunting

The Romans built temples as homes for the gods. Each god or goddess had a temple of their own. It was built in the finest stone, and decorated with statues and carvings.

Apollo, god of the Sun and of the arts

Why did Roman women look pale?

Slaves mixed skin creams from all kinds of ingredients such as flour, chalk, lead, and asses' milk.

Pale skin was a sure sign that a woman came from a rich, noble family. Poorer women had to work outside. Their faces burned in the hot summer sun, and became rough and red in the cold winter winds.

Fashionable men wore perfume and makeup. They even had stick-on leather patches to hide any spots or scars.

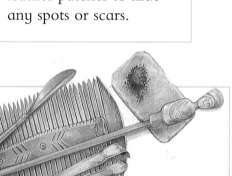

The Romans used all sorts of beauty tools—combs and hairpins made of bone, heated curling tongs, tweezers to pluck out stray hairs, and tiny spoons to scoop the wax from their ears.

Why did Romans hit their hairdressers?

Most Roman noblewomen had two or three slave girls to do their hair. Some of the women were cruel. They jabbed their slaves with a hairpin if the girls tugged their hair—and even whipped them if the style came out wrong.

Wigs were very fashionable. Blond hair came from German slaves. Dark, glossy hair was bought from poor women in India.

Why did Romans wear togas?

Men wore togas for special ceremonies. Wearing one showed that you were a Roman citizen. Slaves weren't allowed to wear a toga. An ordinary citizen had a plain white one, a senator's had a purple trim, and the emperor's was purple all over.

Why did Romans jump in the bath together?

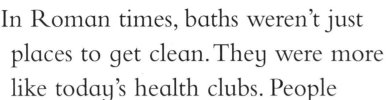

In Roman times, baths weren't just places to get clean. They were more like today's health clubs. People went there to stay fit, play games or sports, meet up with their friends, relax after a hard day's work—and give themselves a good wash, too!

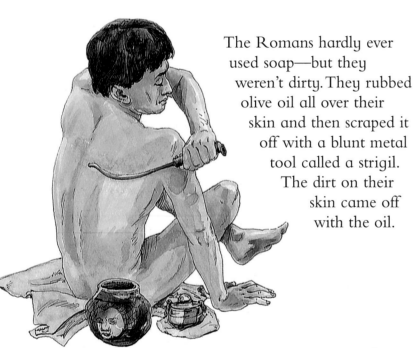

The Romans hardly ever used soap—but they weren't dirty. They rubbed olive oil all over their skin and then scraped it off with a blunt metal tool called a strigil. The dirt on their skin came off with the oil.

Hot air from underground furnaces was used to heat the bath water. But it also made the bottom of the bath very hot, so some people wore sandals so they didn't burn their feet!

Some public baths had a library—very handy for people who liked to read in the bath.

How many people could fit on the toilet?

The Romans didn't go to the bathroom on their own. Sometimes as many as 16 people sat side by side, laughing and chatting with one another. All of the cities had multiseat public restrooms. They were cheap to build, and easy to clean.

ENGAGED

Most homes didn't have a toilet. Families used big pottery jars instead.

Who lived in high-rise apartments?

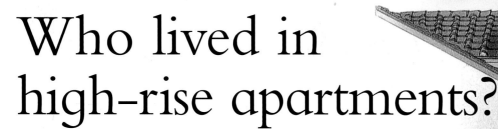

Rome was a crowded city, and short of space. Most ordinary people lived in apartment buildings about six stories high. On the first floor were noisy stores and taverns. At the top were stuffy attic rooms. The nicest apartments were somewhere in the middle.

The Romans liked gardening. Rich people's gardens had pools and fountains. But even the poorest families kept flowerpots on the windowsill.

Roman high-rises were often built so badly that they fell down. To stop the accidents, Emperor Augustus passed a law forbidding any new building being more than 65 feet (20 meters) high.

Which houses had holes in the roof?

Rich people's houses were built around an open-air courtyard. The open roof let in daylight and cool breezes during the summer—but chilly wind and rain in the winter.

Which guard dog was made of stone?

Many Roman homes had a picture of a guard dog near the front door. Like all mosaics, they were made of tiny pieces of stone. The words "CAVE CANEM" (say *cah-vay cah-nem*) meant "Beware of the dog"— to scare off any burglars!

Who brought slaves, spices, and silk?

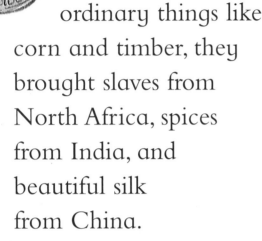

Merchants traveled to the very ends of the empire, and beyond, to bring back goods for the citizens of Rome. As well as ordinary things like corn and timber, they brought slaves from North Africa, spices from India, and beautiful silk from China.

Ostia was the port of Rome. It lay on the coast, 15 miles (25 kilometers) from the city. Sacks of corn and jars of wine and olive oil were stored in warehouses at the port, and sent up to the market by barge.

Most merchants preferred to keep their ships in port all winter, safe from storms and shipwrecks.

To prevent traffic jams, traders and farmers could only bring their goods into Rome at night. With all those noisy carts, it must have been difficult to sleep!

Where was the world's first shopping mall?

Trajan's Forum was a marketplace in Rome's city center. It had 150 stores, brand new offices, and a huge open space where traders could set up their stands. Citizens strolled around the Forum, looking at the goods and gossiping with their family and friends.

Did the Romans eat pizza?

The taverns did a roaring trade selling hot food and drink. Few families had a kitchen at home, and ovens were forbidden in high-rise apartments, for fear of fire.

Every day the Romans bought hot pies and tasty treats, a little like modern pizzas, from the eating houses and taverns in the busy towns. The "pizzas" were topped with onions, fish, and olives—but not tomatoes, which were brought over from South America about 1,500 years later.

In hot weather, rich people cooled their drinks with snow. It was carried down from the mountains by slaves.

22

Why did people vomit at banquets?

At the best banquets, many guests didn't have room for all of the wonderful food and drink. To solve the problem, they would sometimes go outside and make themselves sick. Then they returned to the table to eat some more!

Wealthy Romans ate all types of fancy foods, such as boiled ostrich, or dormice in honey. They also liked surprises. At one banquet, a roast pig was carved open, and a flock of live thrushes flew out!

Who ate lying down?

Wealthy Romans didn't sit up at a table. Instead, they lay propped up on their elbows on long, wooden couches. This must have given them indigestion. Their children had more sense— they sat on stools, close to their parents' couch.

Who went to school in Roman times?

Roman children only studied three subjects at junior school—reading, writing, and sums.

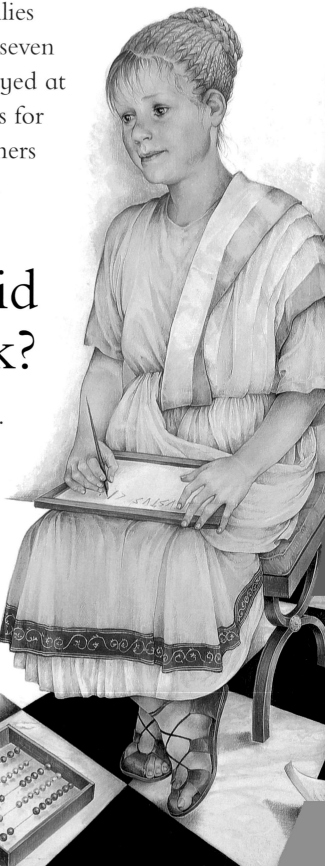

Boys and girls from wealthy families went to school when they were seven years old. But poor children stayed at home. Some of them ran errands for their parents or looked for work. Others played in the street and got into trouble.

What language did the Romans speak?

Everyone who lived in Italy spoke Latin. Everywhere else in the empire, people spoke their own local languages. But there were so many that people from different parts of the empire had to learn Latin, too, so that they could all understand one another!

Girls left school at 11 but boys stayed until they were 16 or 18 years old.

What did the children play with?

Roman children played with all kinds of odds and ends. If they couldn't afford glass or pottery marbles, they used little round nuts instead. They also threw dice made of bones. They even used pigs' bladders—blown up like balloons—to play soccer with!

CAESAR HORRIBILISSIMUS EST

The Romans loved to scribble on walls. On many of their buildings you can still see the rude things they wrote about their leaders, enemies, and even their friends!

The Romans used letters for numbers: I was 1, V was 5, X was 10, L was 50, etcetera.

I, II, III, IV, V, VI, VII, VIII, IX, X, XI, XII, XIII, XIV . . .

Why were Roman roads so straight?

The Romans were excellent engineers. Before they built a road, they used measuring instruments to figure out where the road should go. They chose the shortest, straightest route between two camps, forts, or towns—and destroyed any hedges, buildings, or other obstacles in the way. The roads linked the entire empire.

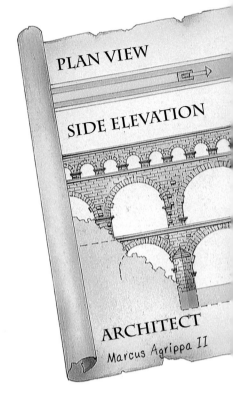

PLAN VIEW

SIDE ELEVATION

ARCHITECT
Marcus Agrippa II

Road builders put milestones along the side of the road so that travelers knew how far they had gone. A Roman mile was 1,000 paces long, about the same as a modern mile (1.6 kilometers).

ROME
500
MILES

The roads had strong foundations. On the bottom, a thick layer of sand was first covered by stones, and then by gravel. On the top was a smooth surface of carefully-fitted paving stones.

Which bridges were always full of water?

CLAUDIUS EMPEROR

Aqueducts look similar to bridges, but instead of a pathway along the top they have a deep channel of water. The Romans built them to carry water from mountain streams to nearby cities. Without aqueducts, the people wouldn't have had their baths, toilets, or fountains of fresh running water.

The Romans invented concrete by mixing lime, water, and the ash from volcanoes. Concrete was as strong as stone, and it set hard even under the water.

The Romans invented arches, too. Each arch rested on a wooden frame until the very last stone, called the keystone, was in place.

Who was thrown to the lions?

The amphitheater in Rome was the Colosseum. It could seat up to 50,000 spectators.

On special days, people flocked to see spectacular shows at the amphitheater. Christians, criminals, and slaves were thrown into a ring with lions to be chased, wounded, and killed. The crowds cheered noisily. They thought it was fun to watch people suffer—but to us it seems wicked and cruel.

Watching men fight was another popular sport. Gladiators were slaves who were sent into the arena to kill animals—or one another—to please the bloodthirsty crowds.

28

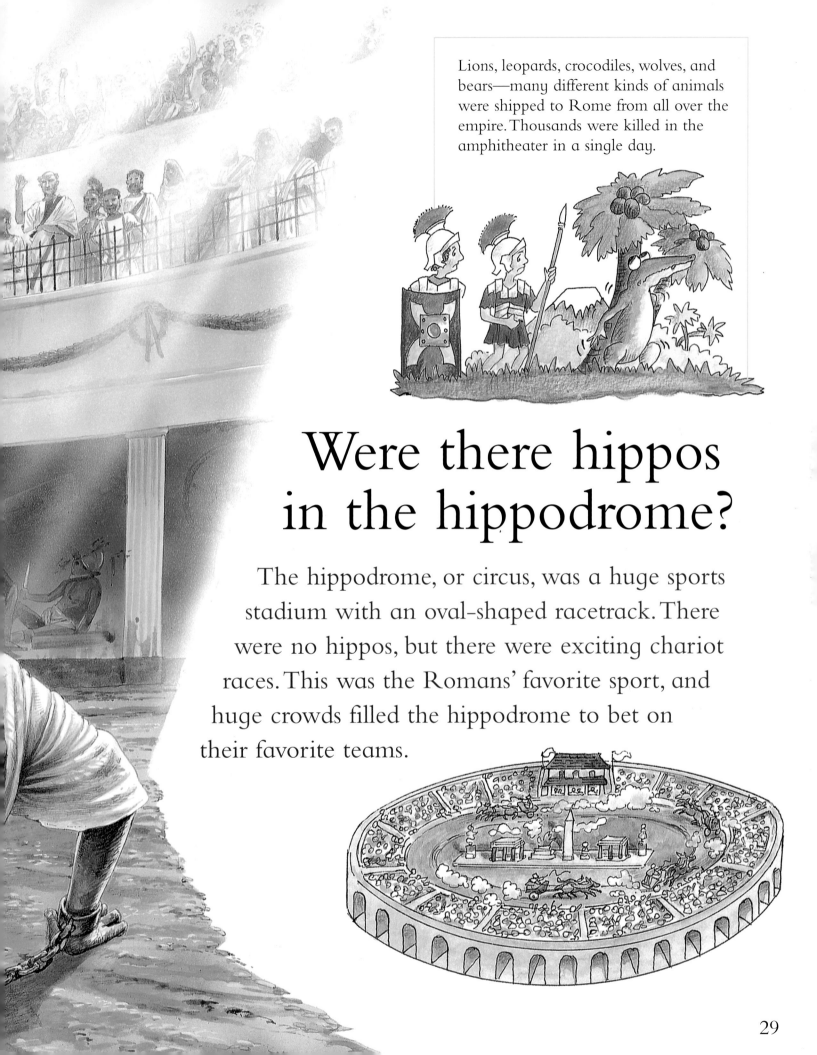

Lions, leopards, crocodiles, wolves, and bears—many different kinds of animals were shipped to Rome from all over the empire. Thousands were killed in the amphitheater in a single day.

Were there hippos in the hippodrome?

The hippodrome, or circus, was a huge sports stadium with an oval-shaped racetrack. There were no hippos, but there were exciting chariot races. This was the Romans' favorite sport, and huge crowds filled the hippodrome to bet on their favorite teams.

Where can you visit a Roman town?

Archaeologists have studied Pompeii since the 1800s, and have uncovered an almost-perfect Roman town.

Pompeii was a bustling town not far from Rome. In the year 79 B.C., a nearby volcano erupted, and buried the town in ash. Pompeii lay hidden for centuries until, one day, some farmers discovered its remains. Today you can visit to see what life was like in Roman times.

MAKING MODELS

1 People were buried by the volcano's ash. Over the years, their bodies rotted away, leaving people-shaped holes in the hardened ash or rock.

2 Archaeologists used the holes as molds. They poured plaster inside, and waited for it to set.

3 Chipping away at the rock left plaster models of the Romans. Archaeologists study these carefully to learn about Roman life.

Mount Vesuvius was an active volcano. As it erupted, showers of ash poured onto Pompeii, killing the people with poisonous fumes.

The Roman empire grew weaker and weaker. It was attacked by warriors from the north and the east, who split up the empire into many small kingdoms.

How do we know about the Romans?

The Roman empire came to an end in the 470s. Yet Roman buildings, mosaics, writings, paintings, and weapons have all survived. Remains like these tell us about the people and the way they lived.

Some Roman finds are peculiar. Archaeologists in London, U.K., have dug up a pair of black leather underpants. Who could have lost them all those years ago?

Index

TITLES IN THE **I WONDER WHY** SERIES

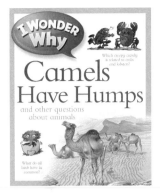

I Wonder Why **Camels Have Humps** and other questions about animals

I Wonder Why **Caterpillars Eat So Much** and other questions about life cycles

I Wonder Why **Countries Fly Flags** and other questions about countries

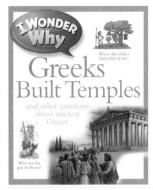

I Wonder Why **Greeks Built Temples** and other questions about ancient Greece

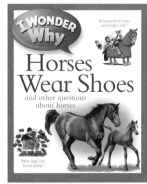

I Wonder Why **Horses Wear Shoes** and other questions about horses

I Wonder Why **I Sleep** and other questions about my body

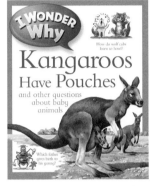

I Wonder Why **Kangaroos Have Pouches** and other questions about baby animals

I Wonder Why **Leaves Change Color** and other questions about plants

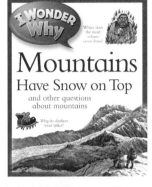

I Wonder Why **Mountains Have Snow on Top** and other questions about mountains

I Wonder Why **Penguins Can't Fly** and other questions about polar lands

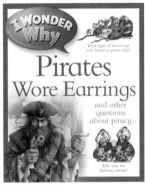

I Wonder Why **Pirates Wore Earrings** and other questions about piracy

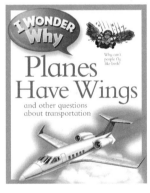

I Wonder Why **Planes Have Wings** and other questions about transportation

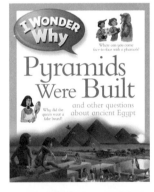

I Wonder Why **Pyramids Were Built** and other questions about ancient Egypt

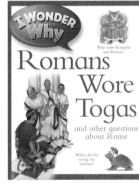

I Wonder Why **Romans Wore Togas** and other questions about Rome

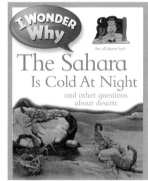

I Wonder Why **The Sahara Is Cold At Night** and other questions about deserts

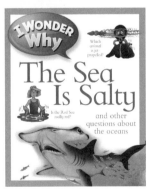

I Wonder Why **The Sea Is Salty** and other questions about the oceans

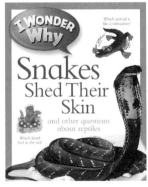

I Wonder Why **Snakes Shed Their Skin** and other questions about reptiles

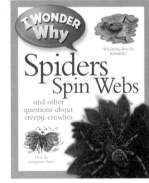

I Wonder Why **Spiders Spin Webs** and other questions about creepy-crawlies

I Wonder Why **Stars Twinkle** and other questions about space

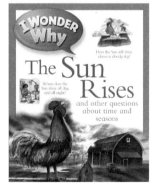

I Wonder Why **The Sun Rises** and other questions about time and seasons

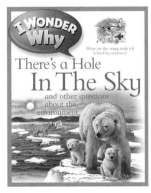

I Wonder Why **There's a Hole In The Sky** and other questions about the environment

I Wonder Why **Triceratops Had Horns** and other questions about dinosaurs

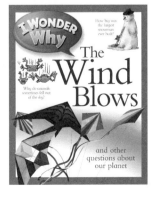

I Wonder Why **The Wind Blows** and other questions about our planet

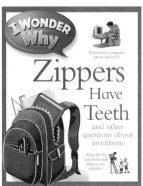

I Wonder Why **Zippers Have Teeth** and other questions about inventions